GIVING
offence

MARTIN ROWSON

LONDON NEW YORK CALCUTTA

Seagull Books 2009

Text and images © Martin Rowson 2009

ISBN-13   978 1 90649 701 9

British Library Cataloguing-in-Publication Data
A catalogue record for this book is available
from the British Library

Typeset and designed by Seagull Books, Calcutta, India
Printed in Calcutta at Rockwel Offset

CONTENTS

James Gillray (1757–1815): Midas Transmuting all into Gold [*scored through*] Paper (1797). *A shortage of gold and a run on the Bank of England, triggered by mounting cost of the war against France, led Prime Minister William Pitt, a frequent target of Gilllray's cartoons, to suspend cash payments and substitute paper money for gold. Pitt is portrayed here as an all-powerful colossus Midas, straddling the Bank of England (resembling a privy), gorged with gold, spewing forth paper money.*

OF TABOOS AND TRANSGRESSIONS

Offence, like beauty, is in the eye of the beholder, which is how we come to know that taking offence is an entirely subjective business. We are different, and for a variety of reasons we have different values, with higher or lower thresholds of tolerance accordingly. That, in itself, is often a source of regret for many people who believe that there is a whole range of human activities or opinions that should be either protected or forbidden because of their capacity to give or take offence. Nonetheless, they can comfort themselves with the thought that at least some human activities or opinions are held to be universally offensive. There is an overwhelming consensus which judges that things like cannibalism, incest, paedophilia, necrophilia or coprophagia are so beyond the spectrum of acceptable behaviour that it's not just offensive to engage in or advocate these vile practices, it's offensive even to mention them.

That's the power of offence. It's about taboos; it's about respecting or transgressing that deep yet vague common notion of what's right and wrong, the kind of ur-morality we all recognize to some degree, even though, like Milton's description of God, it's also a recognition of something that is unperceived but understood.

But that doesn't mean that there aren't individuals or even whole societies or cultures that enthusiastically embrace cannibalism, incest, paedophilia or coprophagia.

In his play *Jumpers* (1974), Tom Stoppard has his hero, the philosopher George Moore, reflect that in some societies they venerate their parents by eating them, while in others the veneration is displayed by buying them a small cottage in the Home Counties. Even so, many people would be deeply offended by the suggestion that there are clearly elements of cannibalism in the Christian celebration of the Eucharist, and they might be even more offended if it were pointed out to them that the epidemic of the disease Kuru among the Fore people of Papua New Guinea—a form of spongiform encephalopathy similar to Creutzfeldt–Jakob Disease, transmitted by prions as a consequence of the Fore's cannibalistic funeral practices—only appeared in the 1950s after the tribe had been converted to Christianity. Failing to grasp the nuances of the new theology, the Fore started scoffing their dead parents' brains in their own, twisted interpretation of the Last Supper.

In the same manner, in order to keep the bloodline pure, incest was central to the dynastic politics of the Egyptian, Persian, Roman and Ottoman empires. Paedophilia, or at least the way we define it today, flourished in the Ancient and Islamic worlds and continues, consensually if furtively, among children themselves. Necrophilia and coprophagia, on the other hand, remain minority enthusiasms, almost always as an adjunct to deeply offensive sexual perversions. That said, there's a widespread myth about Frank Zappa which claims that at a gig one night he called on members of his audience to join him up front and do the most repulsively offensive thing they could imagine, and he promised to outdo them. A young woman duly accepted the offer, and came up and shat on the stage. Zappa then ate the shit.

This takes us to the heart of the matter. Offence, both given and received, hinges on the dynamic conflict between different values, held by different cultures, groups, individuals or generations. We all delineate and define our lives with large and small taboos, and it's the transgression of those taboos that offends us. But in the endless series of dialectical struggles that operate throughout human existence, from the domestic to the global, the transgression of your enemy's taboos is probably the most potent weapon available in your armoury. Moreover, because the taboos themselves are frequently the apparently irrational results of ancient and now obscure social or cultural conditioning, their power lies in their mystery; the taboos are, in practice, part of a deep, dark magic which you defy at your peril. But, for that very reason, transgressing the taboos has an equal or even greater potency, both in damaging your opponents and in asserting your power over them. But, of course, because this is a dynamic process, once the old taboos are torn down, new ones come to replace them, and the potential to give and take offence ratchets upwards and ever onwards.

Forty years ago, the older generation was deeply offended by the hairstyles, dress sense, politics and sexual licentiousness of their children. In turn, the children, in giving offence, were demonstrating how deeply offended they were by their parents' rigidity, complacency, cowardice and conservatism. A mother's deep offence at her daughter's miniskirt was just as likely to be matched by the daughter's deep offence at her mother's fur coat.

(Note, for a moment, the dimensions of offence. It's invariably deep, and never wide or long or thick. This always pertains, even when the offenders are themselves offended by the shallowness of the issue over which the offended have taken offence.)

Most people today are deeply offended by racism, and a belated recognition of the monstrous crimes committed in its name has resulted in racism, in public at least, being one of the dominant taboos of Western society. Yet, a hundred years ago, racism was in the mainstream of European cultural philosophy and, in private and in practice, it maintains a powerful if vestigial virulence. But however half-hearted establishment sponsorship of racism as a taboo may be, these days the onus for taking offence lies with the anti-racists. Until very recently, things were the other way round.

Forty-five years ago, when my mother was fostering babies prior to their adoption (because the circumstances of their births meant they'd broken the taboo against illegitimacy, just as their mothers had broken

the taboo against sex outside marriage),
one day she was wheeling one of the foster
babies down the road in his pram when she
met a friend of hers who, on seeing that the
baby was black, turned it on its stomach to
avoid the possibility of giving offence to
anyone who might imagine that my mother
was guilty of breaking the taboo against
miscegenation. Thirty years earlier, when
racism was still respectable, a German
Brownshirt went to see a Marx Brothers
movie in Berlin, before the Nazis banned
all such films, and laughed and laughed
and laughed. However, on leaving the cin-
ema, someone told him that the Marx
Brothers were Jewish, and he immediately
went to demand his money back, having
been deeply offended at being misled into
watching a film featuring members of a race
whose very existence he found offensive.

Sixty years later, the stand-up comic
and conjurer Jerry Sadowitz was waiting in

the wings at a charity comedy gig when a fellow comedian made a bet with him that he wouldn't dare crack a joke about Nelson Mandela. Mandela's status as a champion in the struggle against apartheid has effectively rendered any criticism of him a taboo in itself, but undeterred Sadowitz went on stage, grabbed the microphone and yelled, 'That Nelson Mandela: what a cunt!' When the uproar that ensued—a mixture of shocked laughter and howls of protest—finally died down, Sadowitz continued, 'The bastard owes me five quid.'

Personally, I align myself with anyone who finds each or all of those examples of racism in action offensive. However, each offence is different, both in practice and purpose. My mother's friend was mostly guilty simply of thoughtlessness, even though this kind of complacency in the face of convention and conformity can often prove to be deadly. The Brownshirt, on the other hand, was more personally culpable, because the source of his offence, as well as his offensive behaviour, lay in his politics. But because the dialectics of politics are just as littered with supposedly inviolable taboos as any other area of human interaction, respect for or transgression of those taboos is an integral part of politics. And so, accordingly, is being both offended and offensive. Nor should we doubt the genuine nature of the offence taken by the Brown-shirt: it's just that he was madly, murder-ously and offensively wrong.

Sadowitz, however, presents us with something altogether different: unlike the other two cases, he wasn't being offensive in retaliation for having been himself offended—he was trying to be funny, just trying to raise a laugh.

I've believed for a long time that hu-mour is a hardwired evolutionary survival tool. Given our species' capacity for cognition, we recognize many things about our individual existence—including the inevitability of its ending—that would drive us mad and have us all screaming in existential terror from the cradle to the grave if we couldn't laugh at them. That's why we laugh at death, sex, other people or, for that matter, the noise made by all this disgusting stuff that pours out of our bodies on a daily basis, the sound of defecation providing evidence of a kind of bedrock of humour present in human beings. After all, one of the first things babies laugh at is when you blow a raspberry at them.

But humour is infinitely more complex and sophisticated than that suggests, although integral to it is that it isn't and shouldn't be treated as if it were. We all know that if you analyse a joke you disable its potency—it stops being funny. That said, we use humour in a vast variety of ways: to diffuse tension, defuse potentially dangerous

15

encounters, reinforce our sense of ourselves
and our control of the world around us.
Thus humour can be used both aggressively
and defensively, typified best by the difference between an Irish and a Jewish joke.
The purpose of the Irish joke is aggressive,
to mock the other; the Jewish joke, on the
other hand, mocks the teller, but by using
humour to reinforce the teller's status and
power through inverted mockery. In other
words, if I can laugh at myself and my mis-
fortune as a defence strategy, I've taken control of both myself and a dynamic in which
you were previously mocking me aggressively in order to exert your control over
me. Which, in turn, means there is a chasm
of difference between the same joke told by
different people, a nuance we probably all
understand without having to be told.

By the same token, it's a common
response to appalling events to tell jokes
about them. Jokes about Biafra in the 1960s

were retold about Bangladesh in the early 1970s, and told again about Ethiopia in the 1980s. When Princess Diana was killed in 1997, famously there was a 'national out-pouring of grief', a spontaneous and collec-tive phenomenon that obsessed the media just as much as Diana's death itself. What wasn't noticed, however, was the simultane-ous outpouring of sick jokes: the difference being that the emoting was public, while the jokes, often told by the same people who'd been weeping in the streets, were exchanged—in the pub or round the office water cooler—in relative privacy.

That in itself is another dimension of how we use humour: it both presumes and creates an intimacy. There are a wealth of good reasons why people advertising for sexual partners in the Lonely Hearts columns are often more concerned about getting someone with a 'Good Sense of Humour' than a stud of enormous sexual prowess who doesn't get a joke. In the most reductionist genetic terms, a capacity to laugh at the changing vicissitudes of life suggests a greater adaptability and, therefore, survivability. But we shouldn't forget what happens when we laugh: we release all those lovely endorphins, the mood altering hormones our bodies have evolved to produce in order to modify our behaviour and ensure survivability, and which, quite simply, make us feel better. So it follows that someone who makes you laugh makes you feel good; you want to associate with them, whether by seeking to have sex with them or paying good money to go to a comedy club.

A 'Good Sense of Humour' is, therefore, a vital social tool. When I was at school in the 1970s, we all knew that there were certain boys whose social skills were either unformed or congenitally absent, so they'd recite entire Monty Python sketches to make us think they had a sense of humour and so we'd like them. In his book *The God Delusion* (2006), Professor Richard Dawkins repeatedly invokes his dead friend Douglas Adams, author of *The Hitch-Hiker's Guide to the Galaxy* (1979), for the same reason.

In 2003, I presented Michael Foot with a cartoon to celebrate his 90th birthday held at the well-known Gay Hussar restaurant in London's Soho. Afterwards, I was standing out on Greek Street talking to a photographer who then asked me for my contact details. As I don't have a business card, I was writing down my e-mail address in my sketchbook, when Alastair Campbell, Tony Blair's director of communications, came out of the restaurant and immediately started shouting at me: 'Isn't that fucking typical? Martin fucking Rowson writing fucking autographs!' When I protested that I was doing nothing of the kind, he went on: 'Course you are, you fucking wanker! You fucking love it!' The point of repeating this story is not to demonstrate once more that Campbell is a foul-mouthed bully, but because I realized, almost instantly, that he was trying to be funny. True, it was more Derek and Clive than Dorothy Parker, but we play the cards we're dealt, and Campbell's coarseness doesn't obviate the fact that, in his heart of hearts, he just wanted me to love him.

Or maybe he wanted me to hate him. Either way, his brutal joviality was intended to elicit some kind of response, both of them equally potent in altering my mood, so he was using either aggression or humour in a standard attempt both to control me and either reinforce or welcome me into some kind of intimacy with him. It probably says more about me than about him that I chose to laugh. But I could, just as easily, have taken deep offence, despite the fact that his true intention may indeed have been to make me laugh.

Objectively, the same could be said of any joke, even if its purpose is to charm and disarm. Objectively, it doesn't matter whether it's a Jew or a non-Jew telling a Jewish joke, if you find all jokes about Jews offensive. Likewise, a gauche and gawky schoolboy could, in reciting Monty Python's Parrot Shop sketch, unexpectedly find himself in deep water if he unwittingly performed it in front of a particularly touchy and recently bereaved parrot-owner. And although the Diana jokes fulfilled a social and psychological function in both releasing tension and reinforcing social bonds just as much as the public displays of grief, there were many people who would have been deeply offended by any mention of Diana that ventured beyond the reverential and the mawkish. I discovered this to my cost at the time.

OFFENCE IS MY BUSINESS

It's my job, as a satirical cartoonist, to give offence. But I need immediately to qualify that statement. I see my job as giving targeted offence, because satire, to borrow H. L. Mencken's definition of journalism, is about comforting the afflicted and afflicting the comfortable. In other words, if I draw rude pictures of people less powerful than myself, what I do ceases to be satire, and creeps into one of the wider spheres of aggressive, bullying humour and into areas I consider offensive.

So, although I'm inclined to think that the non-satirist's standard definition of satire as 'puncturing pomposity' is one of the most pompous phrases in the English language, I buy into it. This is because the urge to mock our social or political betters is something else hardwired into us, to stop us going mad at the injustice of their being held to be superior to us in the first place.

Indeed, it's been argued by several anthro-
pologists that early humans, unlike other
social primates, lived in largely egalitarian
groups, mostly as a result of the equal divi-
sion of labour between the genders involved in hunting and gathering, but where
the status quo was maintained by physically
weaker individuals forming alliances
against the strong and keeping them in
their place through mockery. It was only
later, once agriculture obliged us to live in
settled communities, that the strong seized
the opportunity to impose their will and
power on the rest of us, thus reverting
human beings back to the condition of
baboons.

Perhaps because of this ancient race
memory, mockery of the powerful is as
ubiquitous as humour itself. In political
tyrannies, tolerance of public expression of
this kind of mockery is extremely limited,
and bolstered by thousands of years of

cultural conditioning, itself reinforced by the creation of taboos like blasphemy or *lèse majesté*, themselves closely linked and often interchangeable. Even in less oppressive political circumstances, these taboos endure.

To return for a moment to Diana. You can see in both the tragic and comic responses to her death the interplay of respecting and transgressing both political and religious taboos: on the religious side, there was the death taboo, as well as a kind of attenuated blasphemy when discussing a woman who had been elevated, by both the media and herself, to the status of a lay goddess; and on the political side, the instinctive deference to royalty and, in its way, a trace of the divine right of kings provided other taboos even though, ironically enough, the death of Diana threatened, for a short period, to destabilize the monarchy itself.

Although this whole seething compost of grief, death, religion and politics was riddled with irony, the public recognition of those ironies became a fresh taboo, and not for the first—or last—time it was confidently stated that Diana's death was a catastrophe so great that, once more, Satire—like Diana—was Dead. This meant that almost everything had a heightened capacity to give offence. The post-Diana edition of the satirical fortnightly *Private Eye* contained lengthy satires on the media response to her death, and was pulled from the shelves of the leading newsagent chain WHSmith and many other outlets. The cartoons my colleagues and I drew during this time were subject to much greater editorial scrutiny than usual because of the fear that they might give offence, and I actually had a cartoon pulled by the *Independent on Sunday* from its edition the day after Diana's funeral. Significantly enough, it had nothing to do with Diana, but was the latest in a series of cartoons I produce for that paper's books pages. This one was about the recently deceased US writer William Burroughs, famous for his cut-up technique of writing, and it showed his relatives sitting in a lawyer's office listening to the reading of his will. They were each holding badly wrapped body parts and one relative was saying, 'I'm pleased to see that Uncle Bill stuck with his cut-up technique to the end.' The fact that the cartoon wasn't published was clearly because it was about the wrong death. It was several weeks before I felt I could get away with an even mildly satirical treatment of the whole Diana death phenomenon in a cartoon of 'The New Britain in Touch With Its Emotions' for *Time Out* which showed two tramps sitting in cardboard boxes in Kensington Gardens and wearing smiley masks. One tramp was saying to the other, 'Y'know, I'm getting sick of eating flowers.' By that stage the intensity of national emotion was beginning to dissipate, so I only got a few complaints, but Diana maintains her strange juju power as both manufactured and spontaneous icon, and the only reason I drew a cartoon to mark the 10th anniversary of her death, showing her holed up in a bar in Valparaiso with Mother Teresa of Calcutta, wondering whether she should let Charles in on the joke yet, was because it still had the potential to shock, offend and, therefore, make people laugh.

In the UK, satirists and cartoonists have enjoyed this licence to say the unsayable for centuries, mostly thanks to the new political dispensation that followed on from the Glorious Revolution of 1688, and the new government's failure to renew the Censorship Laws in 1695. The nascent democracy the Revolution produced was based on the idea of religious tolerance—except for Catholics, widely seen as potential terrorists bent on the overthrow of the state—itself a response to the failure to impose religious orthodoxy,

which had resulted in the civil wars of the
1640s and 1650s and the deaths of one
tenth of the population of the British Isles.
In other words, the various warring parties
agreed that, although they'd continue hat-
ing each other, they'd no longer kill each
other. Thus they channelled their hatred
elsewhere, into the Party system, an irre-
sponsible Press and satire. John Locke and
his followers may well have thought that
they were ushering in an Age of Reason, but
1688 also spawned a mushrooming of public satire, with Alexander Pope, Jonathan
Swift and William Hogarth, all the way
through to James Gillray, which ran like a
sewer beneath the Enlightenment. And it
was tolerated because, in this new, experi-
mental, pluralist society, it worked. In the
1780s, the French ambassador to the Court
of St James reported back to Versailles that
he genuinely believed that England was on
the verge of a revolution, on the basis of the

truly offensive cartoons of the Royal Family freely and publicly available from the hundreds of print shops throughout London. But it was, of course, France, where mockery and satire were repressed, unlicensed or private, and where the pressure cooker of resentment finally exploded, that had the revolution.

So, while it may be my job to give offence (and for my part I choose to target that offence at the powerful rather than the powerless), in practice, the whole enterprise is almost ritualistic because satire and satirical cartoons have been established as a valid part of British political discourse for over 300 years. Moreover, the standard template for political cartoons—the caricaturing of real people into an alternative, shape-shifted reality, where they act out a narrative of the cartoonist's devising—was concreted in by Gillray 230 years ago and has remained completely unchanged ever

MONSTROUS CRAWS, at a New Coalition Feast.

James Gillray, Monstrous Craws, at a New Coalition Feast *(1787). One of Gillray's frequent and scabrous attacks on the greed and decadence of the English Royal Family showing King George, dressed as an old woman, the Queen and the Prince of Wales spooning up the contents, representing gold coins, into their mouths. The gate to the state treasury, in the background, is open.*

since. But in some ways, despite its status as a semi-detached part of what used to be called The Establishment, visual satire also exists in the same realm as taboo: it's about deep, dark magic—and not just because caricature can be described as a type of voodoo—doing damage to someone at a distance with a sharp object, albeit in this case with a pen. It's also concerned with control, like all visual art. By recreating the observable or imagined world, that world is synthesized through a human mind, and therefore is tamed through its re-creation, in the same way as the mysteries of human experience are harnessed, re-created and controlled by theatre and literature.

It's an often-repeated cliché that when so-called primitive people first encountered cameras, they believed that their souls were being stolen when their picture was 'taken'. The same is true of caricature, inasmuch as one of the defining factors of

an individual—their physical appearance—
is appropriated by the cartoonist and dis-
torted so that the victim is changed and
altered into something else, far more than
simply a combination of lines on a piece of
paper. Alastair Campbell, once again,
proved the point several years ago when I
drew him from the life as part of a project I
was involved with to caricature the more
celebrated patrons of the above-mentioned
Gay Hussar restaurant. He clearly hated the
whole thing and, unlike my other sitters,
instead of getting on with his lunch he sat
glowering at me and, at one point, shouted
across the restaurant, 'You just won't be able
to stop yourself from making me look like a
really bad person!' My reply was that I draw
what I see. However, the notion that I was,
in some mysterious way, stealing Campbell's
soul, or at the very least wresting control
from him, was confirmed when I presented
him with the drawing for him to sign as a

true record of himself over the course of his lunch. What he did was fascinating, because he instantly clawed back control—over his soul as much as anything else—by saying 'This is a good picture of [Jeremy] Paxman. Now where the fuck's the one of me?' In other words, he denied the power of my dark magic; by insisting it didn't look like him, he was claiming the caricature had failed to 'capture' him, even though it was just a picture, and thereby he disabled the voodoo.

He was right to do so, as all these words like 'taken' or 'capture' confirm. Being caricatured is a transgressive as well as an aggressive act, which is why it's central to political cartooning. Consequently, it's the caricatural dimension of a cartoon that has the potential to give most offence.

To give a further example of this: a couple of decades ago I had a dismal gig at a youth festival the Royal Shakespeare

Alastair Campbell drawn from the life at
THE GAY HUSSAR
21st May 2002

with Fraser Kemp in ¼ profile.
'Freee'

Martin Rowson '02

Company was putting on in Stratford-on-
Avon. One night, as I was leaving the Dirty
Duck Pub through its restaurant, I was
called over to a table by about a dozen or so
young actors, all of whom insisted that I
draw them then and there. I did so, in
exchange for drink, and finally got back to
my guesthouse at about three in the morning. The following lunchtime, I returned to
the pub, shakily in search of a hair of the
dog, but, when I finally caught the attention of the landlady, she leaned across the
bar, grabbed me forcefully by the shoulder
and said, 'Listen, if you come in here with
your sketchpad again, you're not to draw
them however much they ask. I've had
them in tears in here this morning, and it's
more than I can cope with.' Even though,
on this occasion, I'd intended no malice in
my caricatures, there remains something
inescapably malicious about the whole
process of caricature, be it a nose too long

here or a chin too weak there. Again, I put this down to the voodoo, the fact that one person's appearance is filtered through the consciousness of another, and thereby, in some way, stolen.

Politicians recognize this, while also recognizing the established role of cartoons as part of the political discourse, even if it is a ceaseless re-echo of the ancient, primitive and primal politics of our early ancestors mocking putative tyrants in the tribe. By and large, they tend to laugh off—even if they don't laugh at—cartoons of themselves, and maybe even feel flattered that they're sufficiently interesting or important enough to grab the cartoonists' attention; but often they'll also buy the original artwork, which they invariably hang up on their lavatory wall. In other words, through a psychological proximity, they're able to flush away the bad magic of the cartoon along with the rest of the shit, thus neutralizing the offence both given and taken.

And the idea of giving offence is integral to the medium. A cartoon that isn't knocking copy becomes merely propaganda, in that strange reverse transubstantiation that likewise renders a joke that isn't laughed at unfunny. Even when a political cartoon draws back from being deliberately offensive, the ballast the medium brings with it will outweigh the cartoonist's intention.

On 11 September 2001, I was planning to draw a cartoon for the next day's *Scotsman* about Tony Blair visiting the Trades Union Congress Conference in Brighton, when I heard the news that the first plane had struck the World Trade Centre. I then watched the second plane hit the second tower on TV, and spent the rest of the afternoon staring at a blank sheet of paper, wondering how on earth I was meant, as a cartoonist, to respond to the violent and terrible deaths of 3,000 people. I ended up producing a cartoon of a monstrous cloud, shaped like a skull, billowing out from

Lower Manhattan about to snuff out the torch held by the Statue of Liberty, and then phoned my editor to apologize for the cartoon being meaningless and senseless, and he replied that meaninglessness and senselessness were more or less the mood they were after.

Nonetheless, the next day the paper received several complaints because they'd published a cartoon at all. Irrespective of its content, the space on the page carried the subliminal message to the readers that this was a cartoon, and therefore funny, and therefore offensive. Other cartoonists fared far worse than me, having their work pulled or, in one instance, being told to cover another topic (there were no other topics). It seems that although 9/11 was the most visual event in human history, repeated over and over again on television and with every newspaper in the UK devoting pages and pages to photographs of the attacks

and their aftermath, the one visual medium
that instantly became intolerable because of
its capacity for offence was the cartoon. But
once again, the difference lies in the execu-
tion: television images and photographs
may consequently be subject to human
intervention, but they are 'captured'—that
word again—by machines; cartoons, on the
other hand, are the sole creation of human
beings wielding primitive tools, who create
or re-create reality by filtering it through
their human minds. The process is too
human, too raw sometimes to be entirely
bearable.

Worse still, its readers receive a cartoon,
just as any other image, in a different way
from the way they receive text. A cartoon
isn't, as such, 'read' at all, because reading
is a slow, linear process of nibbling information as you work your way down the column
over a period of minutes, while a cartoon—
often squatting like a gargoyle on top of the

column—is swallowed whole in seconds. Worse than that, on top of being intrinsically different from a machine-made photograph, a cartoon is a piece of polemical journalism, which also makes it different from an illustration. Given the visceral way a cartoon is consumed, straight from the eye to the reptile brain, it's unsurprising that the response is often equally visceral. And the offence, freely given, is duly received.

BITING BACK

Although I use offence as just part of my satirical armoury—to express outrage or to trigger a shock of laughter—I often get as good as I give. Which brings me back to that point about offence being in the eye of the beholder.

Offence is a response, but it's also a tactic. Unlike Sadowitz, I rarely produce cartoons merely in order to offend for offensiveness' sake. Instead, it's to make a point, often in reaction to something of itself far more offensive. As such, I'm expressing an opinion, albeit visually and weirdly, but as part of the wider political discourse. But this is where offence comes into its own.

In the past, I may well have produced some genuinely offensive cartoons, like the one I drew for *Time Out* after a biography of Princess Diana revealed that she suffered from bulimia, depicting her vomiting over the bow of a ship being launched with a flunkey in the background saying, 'The real bugger of it is trying to get her to eat a bottle of champagne during lunch . . .'

Many of *Time Out*'s readers were proba-bly quite justified in taking offence, although the calls for me to be publicly castrated were, perhaps, over-egging the pudding. In admittedly hopelessly disingenuous mitiga-tion I'd say that I think the joke was quite

funny, and that public figures—in other
words, people more powerful than me—are
fair game, and can always retire to private
life if they want to break the contract
between themselves, the public, the media
and me. I was also rather heartened by a
letter published a week after the first del-
uge of hate-mail, whose writer, herself
bulimic, thought my cartoon was very funny
and had cut it out and stuck it on her
fridge.

Other cartoons have been more directly
political, but have excited equal outrage. A
drawing I did for the *Sunday Tribune* in
Dublin at the time of the 1992 UN Population Conference in Cairo, prior to which
the Pope had entered into a tactical alliance
with the Ayatollahs of Iran, resulted in the
Tribune's offices being picketed by nuns and
members of Opus Dei. Then again, I had
drawn the Pope standing at the Conference
reception desk, flanked by bearded mullahs

holding 'Death to Rushdie' placards and
stoning women delegates, saying 'Hellow!
We are the Pro-Life delegation!' After Pope
John Paul II's death, I drew a rather sweet
cartoon for the *Guardian* of the Pope being
escorted across a heavenly cloudscape by
the Grim Reaper, who's saying to him,
'What do you mean? Am I pro-life?' That
got a few complaints, but none as baroque
as the one inspired by a relatively innocu-
ous cartoon, which the reader said was the
most offensive, vile, repellent, calculated to
offend, disgusting (and on he went, having
clearly got out his thesaurus) cartoon or
image to have appeared in any paper or
publication 'since the foundation of the
state!' Along the way I've also been reported to the Press Complaints Commis-
sion by one man who considered a marginal
gag written in tiny letters on a fax in the
body of the cartoon ('The Pope is Catholic.
The Blairs shit in the woods') a grossly

offensive intrusion into the private life of
the then Prime Minister, and by a supporter
of the Animal Liberation Front (ALF) who
was deeply offended by my comparing the
ALF to the Continuity IRA after the
Omargh bombing.

These were minor disruptions to my
peace of mind. It was only after the
Guardian started to publish my cartoons on
their website that I discovered how truly—
and, of course, deeply—offensive I could
really be. Starting with a cartoon suggesting
that the 2004 US Presidential Election
would result almost immediately in a new
American Civil War between the Christians
and the Constitutionalists ('Death to the
Gay Abortionists!'), followed by George
Bush, Condoleeza Rice and Donald Rums-
feld in Nazi armbands emblazoned with
crosses instead of swastikas, a cartoon of
Bush crossing Canal Street in New Orleans
pastiching the famous painting of Washing-

ton crossing the Delaware, Bush and the
Chinese President shaking their blood-
soaked hands and discussing White Phos-
phorous and many other cartoons on
Bush's presidency and Iraq, I regularly
received hundreds and hundreds of hate
e-mails.

My correspondents were clearly deeply
offended by my cartoons, and many had
been alerted to my offence by websites re-
producing them. And as my intention had
been to offend, I couldn't really complain if
people duly were. But the strange thing was
how offensive the responses were themselves. One started: 'When you've finished
scraping the maggots out of your whore-
mother's cunt,' and went on to describe in
detail how I regularly rape my children, but
only after I've tired of raping Arab boys.
Another said I was 'dumber than an Irish
cunt'. Most limited themselves to telling me
that I was a dumb limey asshole who'd be

STRIP SEARCH by Martin Rowson

It is *typical* of cynical OLD EUROPEANS that they dismiss the *UNITED STATES* of *AMERIKA* as a *benighted land totally bereft of a SENSE of IRONY*... However, as with *EVERYTHING ELSE*, in Irony terms America *leads the world!*

For starters, we all know that Amerika is a *vibrant, classless, democratic* REPUBLIC, so is obviously run by **PLUTOCRATIC ARISTOCRATS** who know that it is their DESTINY to **REIGN LIKE KINGS!**

(Although they also know that, despite believing in DIVINE RIGHT, they also have to be elected, usually, so the aristos pretend to be ordinary *dumb slobs* like the electorate — see fig.1)

Fig.1

ONE THINGY I LEARNIFIED AT YALE IS THAT I'M JUST AN *ORDINARY DUMB JOE JUS'* LIKE ALL THE OTHER LIDDLE GUYS OUT THERE, AN' VEESY VERSO!

A *deeper Irony* arises here. Although DESTINED to be KINGS, the aristos don't actually believe in Government, as it gets in the way of all that vibrant classless (but not necessarily *democratic*) stuff (fig.2) ———

BUT! A KING needs a KINGDOM (*Texas* won't quite do) even if you don't intend to do anything apart from executing poor blacks when you come into your BIRTHRIGHT and become KING. This makes it all very confusing...

Fig.2

WHADJA MEAN, THERE'S A LAW SAYIN' DAD'S FRIENDS CAN'T MELT GREENLAND AND SELL IT BACK TO THE ESKIMOVIANS AS BATH WATER?

DON'T WORRY, JUNIOR! WE'LL NUKE ANTARTICA INSTEAD!

Worse, you can only *fuck* over the Economy & line the pockets of your Plutocratic Aristocrat buddies for SO LONG before your subjects start thinking you're a BAD KING! BUT, if you do anything to improve the lives of your subjects you will become, by your own lights, a TYRANT (fig.3)

AN' WE MIGHT DO SOMETHIN' 'BAHT HEALTHCARE AN' SCHOOLS AN' ALL, BUT PROBABLY NOT...

GODDAM! THIS COUNTRY IS TURNIN' INTO NAZI GERMANY!

Fig.3

IRONIC? I THOUGHT THEY WERE NEXT! AIN'T WE STILL DEALIN' WITH THE IRAQICS?

And thus the only option left to you, in order to uphold those FOUNDING (and clearly *ironic*) PRINCIPLES of democracy, liberty and all that old guff so that they shall not *perish* from the Earth is to become EMPEROR of a CONQUERED and RESENTFUL WORLD as a classic DISPLACEMENT ACTIVITY so that your impoverished and neglected subjects can democratically elect you (if absolutely necessary) to be KING BY DIVINE RIGHT. *Ironic, huh?*

@Martin Rowson '03

speaking German if it weren't for the USA, and would soon be speaking Arab after the Islamist takeover of Europe. One person even enrolled me, without my knowledge, on a gay dating website and I got several mystifying inquiries from interested parties in Florida before I discovered their source and cancelled my unconscious membership.

My friend and colleague Steve Bell receives even more of this trash than I do, but sensibly observes that if these idiots are writing bilious e-mails to him, they're too busy to do anything truly dangerous. However, mixed up in all this Tourettic spleen were several fairly plausible death threats. Things got worse after I produced a cartoon for the *Guardian* during Israel's disastrous incursion into Lebanon in the summer of 2006. It was, I concede, a brutal cartoon, commenting on brutal events, and perhaps I should have painted the Stars of David blue on the knuckledusters on an

Israeli fist smashing a Lebanese child's face while missing a Hezbollah hornet, to make it quite clear that I was referring to the flag of the State of Israel rather than the symbol of worldwide Jewry. I doubt, however, that it would have made much difference, not least because the presence of the Star of David on the Israeli flag is there precisely in order to claim to represent Jews everywhere. The equation of Israel and Jewry has proved to be a brilliant tactic to disarm Israel's critics, simply by calling any criticism of Israel and its actions anti-Semitic. In the thousands of e-mails I received, again mostly fomented through various websites, the message in all of them can be more or less distilled down to, 'Fuck off you anti-Semitic cunt.' And as a tactic, it worked. I was deeply shaken by being accused of something I'm not, although I eventually worked out that the heart of the insult lay in the word 'anti-Semite' rather than any of the others, because insults usually work best when they accuse you of being something you're not. Otherwise they're not insults, merely statements of fact. But long before this incident, I'd got used to receiving complaints whenever I drew Ariel Sharon, that I'd produced the most anti-Semitic cartoon since the closure of Julius Streicher's notorious Nazi hate-sheet *Der Stürmer*. Again, the offensiveness of the response seemed to outweigh the original offence. All I'd done was caricature a fat, Jewish-looking man in a stupid drawing, in no more exaggerated a way than I'd depict anyone. Yet, as a consequence, I ended up being compared with the principle cheerleader of the Holocaust.

The disproportionate nature of these responses—the obscenity and the death threats—pales in comparison to the response to the cartoons of Prophet Muhammad published by the Danish paper *Jyllands-Posten* in October 2005, which five months later resulted in worldwide protests, the burning down of several Danish diplomatic buildings and the deaths of up to a hundred people, even though they were all Muslims, shot dead in the streets of their Muslim countries by Muslim policemen and soldiers after having been incited to riot by Muslim clerics. In this infamous affair, it's clear that *Jyllands-Posten* set out deliberately to offend, as part of the newspaper's long-standing campaign against immigrants, recruiting the voodoo powers of the medium to damage, or at least discomfort, a group of isolated, beleaguered, powerless and poor people in Danish society, some of whom probably also clean the lavatories and empty the bins at *Jyllands-Posten*'s offices. Because they targeted people less powerful than themselves, *Jyllands-Posten*'s cartoons failed my personal Mencken test, and I concluded that the commissioning of the cartoons was wrong, even though the response—by powerful Danish mullahs, let

Typical vehemently anti-Semitic cartoon from Julius Streicher's weekly Nazi paper Der Stürmer *(literally, 'The Stormer'; more accurately, 'The Attacker'). After World War II, Streicher was found guilty of inciting the Germans to exterminate the Jews and was hanged.*

alone the Saudi and Syrian governments—
almost justified them in retrospect.

But it's worth reflecting on the purpose
of all these reactions, whether from Muslims to the Danish cartoons, or the response to my cartoons by Muslims, Zionists,
neo-cons, Americans in general, Catholics,
Serbs, Spaniards or any of the other groups
I've apparently offended over the years,
including some atheists who judged a cartoon I drew of Richard Dawkins for *New
Humanist* magazine to reveal me as deeply
homophobic, because I'd drawn him bang-
ing his wrists together in glee, and wearing
sandals. But while I don't doubt that all
these people are truly, deeply offended,
and have every right to be, rights, despite
any amount of wishful thinking, are merely
assertions. In the Babel of conflicting
human opinions, the right to be offended
works out, in practice, as just another tactic
to win an argument by compelling your

STRIP SEARCH by Martin Rowson

③ XILE! — whether its motivation be *flight* or the yearning to breathe free, throughout HISTORY humans have *upped tents* to seek richer or safer pastures, leaving HOME to find refuge in a new, renewing yet unfamiliar home. And yet, and yet... the *umbilical cord* EVER TWANGS, and shallow roots persistently recall those *deeper, distant* roots, bifurcating into the rich, chthonic *earth* of the ORIGINAL HOMELAND —— So, what if we make a *dream come true* and let **EVERYBODY GO HOME ??!?**

④ ...as mighty ships traverse the World's Oceans, taking home the *immigrant* populations of AMERICA, AUSTRALIA, SOUTH AFRICA, NORTHERN IRELAND, PITCAIRN ISLAND, etc...

BUT MOM! WHERE THE HELL **IS** RUTHENIA?

BACK IN MY OLD DAHOMEY I HOME!

⑦ With the *AMERICAN LANDMASS* now safe for *buffalo* to graze, EUROPE, AFRICA & ASIA are *heaving* — IRELAND sinks under the weight of returning *sons & daughters* of ERIN, while the Welsh & Cornish exercise their *"right to return"* to the abandoned estates of the departing ANGLES, SAXONS & JUTES... Ethnic clashes at airports everywhere... CHINESE claim *en masse* to be a lost tribe of Israel, leading to enormous tailbacks on the Hebron by-pass....

YOU SAID IT, PAL...

② At first, of course, the craven jackanapes of FORTRESS EUROPE'S Interior Ministries are cock-a-hoop as they empty those DETENTION CENTRES...

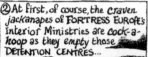

BYE BYE! DON'T FORGET TO WRITE!

NO READMITTANCE

③ But this dream goes much much further... Soon half of Britain's CABINET are back home in crude peat bothies north of the border...

OCH AYE THE NOO!

SHUT UP GORDON!

⑤ And *half measures* DON'T APPLY, so before they can enjoy the wide & empty prairie that was once Detroit, the NATIVE AMERICANS get back across that landbridge to SIBERIA...

SO WHERE DO WE BUILD THE CASINOS?

⑥ Meanwhile, the Israelis return from whence they came. (This entails a short weekend stop in the Bronx, then Kiev, before going back to ISRAEL — oops!)

THE FLIGHT BACK HOME LEAVES IN 20 MINUTES! WE DON'T HAVE TIME TO BUILD SETTLEMENTS ALL OVER UKRAINE!

ANTI-SEMITE!

⑧ Until the yearning itch to go home leads the ENTIRE HUMAN RACE to return to Africa's RIFT VALLEY.

ISN'T IT GREAT FOR US ALL FINALLY TO BE HOME?

EXCEPT THAT HALF THE POPULATION OF BRAZIL IS STANDING ON MY FOOT...

⑨ Everything thus sorted out, a brief word from our sponsors...

HEY CHICO! PEOPLE SAY I'M MAD BECAUSE I LIVE IN A TENT!

BOSS! YOU'RA NO MAD!

I'M A NOMAD! THAT'S WHY I LIVE IN A TENT!

opponent to shut up because what they say is offensive. Special interest groups, whether motivated by politics, religion or anything else, constantly seek to create new taboos to make them, their attitudes and their opinions inviolable, so that all criticism is rendered not just unspeakable but unsayable.

This totalitarian imperative to be freed from the threat of being offended has operated throughout human history. Gods, kings and dictators, in addition to their followers, have all demanded that they be allowed to control other people's thoughts and behaviour to save them from the terrible pain of their feelings being hurt. Doubtless trainspotters would insist on the same privilege, and enjoy the same freedom from mockery, if they thought they could get away with it. With repulsive regularity, the penalty for transgressing taboos and giving offence has been death or the threat of it, even though it should be blindingly obvious to everyone who's ever lived that the most offensive thing anyone can ever do to anyone else is kill them.

That said, there are other kinds of damage that can be wrought, and cartoons, as a subset of mockery, are capable of doing more damage than a lot of other things. That, to a large extent, is their purpose. That damage can either be benign, as I'd insist that my work is, keeping the powerful in check, or malignant, as in the case of the *Jyllands-Posten* cartoons or the anti-Jewish hate cartoons that *Der Stürmer* really did publish. They are, consequently, as offensive as you wish them to be, depending on your point of view. They're also part of that deep, dark magic that defines the taboos we create, which in their turn inform our propensity to give and take offence. But you can invoke that magic in all sorts of different ways.

After my Lebanon cartoon appeared, the *Guardian* published a letter from the Israeli ambassador in London (which pulled the usual trick of equating criticism of Israel with anti-Semitism) that started in an interesting way—by giving a dictionary definition of a cartoon. By this light, he argued, not only was my cartoon offensive, it wasn't even a cartoon. I'm used to the formulation 'so-called' qualifying my critics' description of my cartoons, along with assertions at how badly I've drawn them, but this was something new. What he was saying was that he disagreed with my cartoon, but as a consequence not only pleaded being offended to make me shut up but also asserted that, in its own terms, it didn't even exist. Now that's smart magic.

For, while offence may be in the eye of the beholder, you must never rule out the option of simply blinking and looking away.

INDEX
ON CENSORSHIP

Index on Censorship is Britain's leading organisation promoting freedom of expression. Our award-winning magazine and website provide a window for original, challenging and intelligent writing on this vital issue around the world. Our international projects in media, arts and education put our philosophy into action.

For information and enquiries go to <u>www.indexoncensorship.org</u>, or email enquiries@indexoncensorship.org